Dumfries

Through the Lens
Glimpses of old
Annan Burgh

Dumfries and Galloway
Libraries, Information and Archives
with the Friends of Annandale and
Eskdale Museums 2003

First published 2003
© Publication copyright Dumfries and Galloway Council.

Designed by Dumfries and Galloway Libraries, Information
and Archives. Set and printed by Solway Offset Services,
Catherinefield Industrial Estate, Dumfries for the publisher.

Dumfries and Galloway Libraries, Information and Archives
Central Support Unit, Catherine Street
Dumfries DG1 1JB
Tel: 01387 252070   Fax: 01387 260294
www.dumgal.gov.uk/lia

ISBN 0 946280 61 4
Annan is number 24 in the
Dumfries and Galloway: Through the Lens series.
For a full list of our publications contact us at the above address.

ACKNOWLEDGEMENTS

Rene Anderson, William Anderson, Doris Bone,
Eric Johnstone, George Chalmers, Barbara Edgar,
Beryl Frood, Jim Grant, Jim Hawkins, Jim Irving,
John Irvine, Mamie Lamont, Isabelle Latimer,
Betty McQuade, John Nicholson, Alan Pearcey,
Tom Proudfoot, William Richardson, Ernie
Robinson, Billie Simpson Smith, Bob Thomson,
John Thomson, Wellwood Barton, Vena White,
Joyce Whittington, Alan Wilkins, Gordon Wright,
Annandale Observer, Ronald McLean and the staff
of Annan Library, Anne Ramsbottom of the Annan
Historic Resources Centre, Friends of Annandale
and Eskdale Museums.

INTRODUCTION

Although the banks of the River Annan had attracted Iron Age farmers, Romans and early Christians, it was the powerful Norman dynasty of the Bruces who brought prominence and burgh status to the settlement by the early ford, where Robert de Brus' motte and bailey can still be seen.

The Solway Firth was a natural barrier against invaders during war, and a hindrance to commerce in peaceful times. Annan's location on the first fordable part of the Solway Firth was of great importance both as a route for invading armies and for traders. Because of its position the town suffered from attack and counter attack during the War of Independence and later when "border reiving" was a way of life. In recognition of the town people's resistance and loyalty, a charter was granted to Annan by King James V in 1538; this may have been a renewal of an earlier award. The town's Royal Burgh status was reaffirmed in 1612 by King James VI. Each year the Royal Burgh of Annan celebrates the granting of the charter by Riding the Marches to check that the boundaries are secure. This tradition now stretches back over about 500 years.

After hundreds of years of cross-border conflict, peace was finally achieved. As agriculture developed, Annan became a prosperous market town with coastal shipping links with Liverpool and other industrial towns. This trade was further developed with the coming of the railway in the 1840s. From the beginning of the 18th century the district's children were provided with several schools teaching a range of both classical and practical subjects. In 1802 Annan Academy, which was promoted by the town council, taught a variety of vocational subjects including mathematics, physics and natural science. Lieutenant-General Alexander Dirom (1757-1830), who lived on the Mount Annan estate, was an enlightened land owner. He was responsible for developing agriculture and industry and was also involved with improving roads and having river bridges built. In 1811 with others he promoted the opening of the Annan branch of the newly formed Commercial Bank of Scotland. Annan's 19th century industries, agriculture, fishing, shipbuilding and sandstone quarrying, were later augmented by water mills and wind mills which powered cotton manufacturing, and cereal milling. Bacon curing and tanning were also of vital importance. Agricultural development was supported by factories making bone meal and fertilisers. The town's fine sandstone buildings and bridges are a testimony to the industry and skills of the 18th and 19th century quarrymen and masons.

In 1899 Cochran and Co. established an engineering factory building small ships and a wide range of boilers. The Great War, the 1930s industrial depression years and the Second World War caused many changes in local industries and social attitudes. The building of the nuclear power station at Chapelcross in 1957 resulted in a further influx of people with new skills and outlooks.

Today Annan still has many people employed in the engineering industry in both manufacturing and maintenance, and the two large food-processing companies employ more than 1,000 people. In common with other local communities, improved road transport and the proximity of large superstores has had a detrimental effect on local small traders.

Only a few of the photographs in this collection have been published before. Among the rest are some remarkable and unique ones of great importance, mostly found by chance in old houses or boxes of family memorabilia. Criminally, the extensive photographic archives of the skilled professional photographers of Annan – Irving, Brown, Gibbs and others – were destroyed by those who took over their premises. It is therefore important that all photographs of the Burgh's past are recorded; they should be brought to the attention of the Curator at the Historic Resources Centre, Annan (tel. 01461 201384) so that copies or the originals can be kept in the archives.

Particular thanks are due to both Jim Hawkins and Alan Wilkins without whom this book would not have been.

CARLYLE'S PLACE
In 1899 Carlyle's Place was a fashionable residential area. Number 18 was the home of William Johnstone, a master mason who worked on the construction of the railway stations and bridges at Annan and Cummertrees. In 1922 twenty-four families lived in this street.

BRIDGE HOUSE

According to *Historic Scotland*, Bridge House is one of the finest Georgian houses in a Scottish town; it was built as a hotel in 1780. During the period 1802 to 1820 it served as Annan Academy. Thomas Carlyle and Edward Irving were pupils there, and Carlyle returned as a mathematics teacher. It is planned to refurbish Bridge House as a museum and community centre. The photograph was probably taken before 1900. The occupants of the buildings on either side are listed in the 1898 Trades Directory as the Misses Rae, 5 High Street, nurserymen and seedsmen, and Robert Smith, 11 High Street, general merchant.

HIGH STREET

This aerial view of Annan High Street in 1927 shows the graveyard behind the Town Hall, and Bridge House and its garden. The scene is virtually unchanged today except that Baird's shops have been replaced by a new entrance to Port Street, and part of the graveyard has been built over. In the 1920s the town's prosperity depended on the main employers, Cochran's engineering works, Robinson's cereal mills and fishing. At this time sandstone quarrying was in decline due to high export tariffs.

ST JOHN'S ROAD

This image dates from 1910, and shows Greenknowe Church in the distance beside the railway station. The fine sandstone houses were constructed over a period of several years by Kerr and other local builders. Kerr's own house, 1 St John's Road, was built in 1864, Ravenswood House in 1880. Services in the church ceased in 1930 when St Andrew's Church and Greenknowe merged. The building was converted into the Caledonian Motor Omnibus Company's garage, but in May 1939 the garage and seven omnibuses were destroyed in a disastrous night time fire. For some inexplicable reason no-one called the Annan Fire Brigade. Seven firemen from Dumfries turned up, but without their appliance which was being repaired; they had to use the inadequate Annan fire equipment which *looked more like a window cleaner's.* By chance a plumber in the crowd knew where the nearest hydrant was, but the lid was sealed by the over-zealous application of tar and a road roller. The Dumfries firemen had to smash the lid with a sledge hammer, but they were in time to prevent the fire reaching the large underground fuel tank. *A considerable crowd gathered in various stages of dress and undress, and one lady viewed the conflagration from... the steps of the Central Hotel in a brilliant pink gown, which scintillated in the flickering light.* (Annandale Observer, May 12, 1939).

5

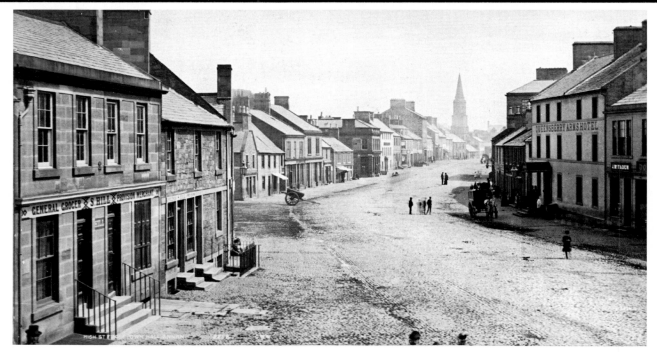

HIGH STREET

An early photograph dating from about 1870, looking east towards the Parish Church. The only traffic is the local stage coach waiting outside the Queensberry Hotel and a farm cart parked on the opposite side of the street. At this time Annan had gas street lighting which was introduced in 1838. Town scavenging followed in 1856. Unlike Dumfries, Annan did not suffer outbreaks of cholera. In Dumfries the disease killed 550 people in 1832 and 450 in 1848. In 1832 two visitors from Dumfries were already ill with cholera when they arrived in Annan, but a set of basic hygiene rules was enforced and the disease was contained. Later a typhoid outbreak in Greencroft Wynd in 1864 cast doubts on the purity of the town's many wells, and a piped public water supply was provided in 1881. In 1883 a public bath house was operated in Rose Street by a Mr Pollock. In 1882-83 the High Street was resurfaced with 4 inch whinstone setts at a cost of £3,500, paid for by public subscription.

PORT STREET

Looking northwards up Port Street in the 1890s, from the first floor window of 19 Port Street. The Georgian gabled warehouse and the late Victorian house on the corner were recently demolished. The warehouse was a rare example of the type which had accommodation on the ground floor. On the right edge of the photograph is the Albert Hall, which was built by James McLean in 1872 and could accommodate 600 people. James had established a cattle mart here in 1870; he was joined by John Thomson in 1880. Cattle drovers from Galloway heading to Huntingdon for the London market passed through Annan until 1863. The smells from the Port Street tannery, bonemeal and manure mills and bacon curing were the subject of complaints in 1865. Bacon curing, once an important industry, was in decline by 1874.

WATER-WORKS INSPECTION
The annual summer inspection of the town's water works at Middlebie was the excuse for a Town Council jaunt in 1905. Note the four-in-hand horse-drawn charabanc, and the food and drink hampers from Annan family grocer and provision merchant J E McJerrow & Co., who had a shop at 57 High Street.

OPENING OF THE PUBLIC LIBRARY

Although the town already had several lending libraries, the opening of the new Public Library in Bank Street in 1906 was a great occasion which attracted large crowds. The photograph records the contrast between the bareheaded dignitaries and the hats and clothes of the townsfolk. The building of the library was funded by Andrew Carnegie who made a fortune with railway and steel investments in the USA. Originally a poor Scots immigrant, he returned to his native country and used part of his wealth to finance free public libraries across the world. Today the building houses Annan's Historic Resources Centre.

ANNAN OLD TOWN HALL

This plain but distinguished building was erected in about 1723. When it was demolished before the building of the present Town Hall in 1878, the massive foundations of Annan Castle were unearthed. Annan Castle was a fortified tower, and was also used as a church before the Parish Church was built in 1790.

10

WULL ANDERSON

Seen here in 1934, Wull was a salmon dealer whose home was Lochfield at the Howgill (pronounced Hogul). He took his cart and fish scales onto the Annan Merse at Summergate after each tide to meet the poke and haaf net fishermen. After boxing and packing the salmon with ice, he took them to Annan Railway Station labelled for London's Billingsgate fish market.

LOUDON FAMILY

The Loudon family were tailors and clothiers. They also sold fishing rods, fishing tackle and river fishing licenses from this house, 25 Port Street. The plaster cast of the salmon was made from a 50½ pound (22.9 kg) fish caught in the River Annan in 1893 by Peter Loudon. Miss Jean Loudon is on the left of the photograph and Peter is in the centre with his brother Jim on the right. Peter was the manager of Hardie Brothers' Edinburgh fishing tackle shop. He was drowned in the River Earn near Crieff in the 1930s when playing a large fish.

SOLWAY VIADUCT

The first sod was cut in 1865 and the viaduct was opened in 1869. Although it was badly damaged by ice flows during the winter of 1880/81 it was fully repaired. The traffic in iron ore between the West Cumberland mines and the Lanarkshire steel works was failing by 1886, and the railway line, never a financial success, was closed to all traffic in 1921 when further expensive repairs were required.

SOLWAY VIADUCT DEMOLITION
The viaduct was used as an unofficial route to Bowness by walkers and cyclists before dismantling commenced in 1934. In 1935 three demolition workers were drowned when their boat was caught by the fast tide and capsized. These are unique photographs taken in 1937 during the final stages of demolition. Today the sandstone piers are the workers' only memorials.

ANNAN HARBOUR

After the railway line was opened in 1848, most goods and passenger traffic went by train, and Annan harbour lost much of its coastal shipping. This photograph, taken at the Annan quay in about 1890, is of typical coastal schooners and a steamer which transported cereals, manure, slates and cement for the Welldale warehouses. T & G Tweedie, whose premises are seen on the right, were manufacturers of agricultural fertilisers.

LAUNCH OF THE "SARAH NICHOLSON"

The launch in 1865 of the clipper *Sarah Nicholson* of 934 tons. The two ladies may be Sarah Nicholson and her mother, possibly still wearing black in mourning for Queen Victoria's husband Albert who died in 1861. This was the last large ship launched by Nicholsons of Annan. After launching, the larger Nicholson ships were towed on the same tide by steam tug to Liverpool for rigging. This newly discovered photograph is labelled WE Irving, photographer, Annan. The Annandale Observer records that WE Irving also photographed William Ewart MP cutting the first sod to mark the start of the construction of the Solway Viaduct in 1865, but no copy of this photograph has been found.

D & T HILL'S SHOP

A newly discovered photograph of D & T Hill's shop at Bridge End House in 1929. The poster in the window advertises the *Annan & District Agricultural Society's Annual Show in Newby Park on Saturday 27th July, 1929, with horses, cows, sheep, pigs etc… Music by Annan Town Band from One o'clock.* The shop displays a wonderful variety of goods including HP Sauce and Tomato Ketchup, Rowntrees Cocoa, Carr's Hungarian Flour, Carr's biscuits, MP Creamy Toffee, Old Calabar Chicala, and Hudson's Soap. Country Butter is chalked up at 1/6 per lb, Country Eggs at 1/8, Finest Cheese at 1/3, and Pure Lard at 9d. The shop is now occupied by Hann & Co., Solicitors.

17

ANNAN CO-OPERATIVE SOCIETY SHOP
Annan Co-op staff outside the extensive frontage of their shop in the 1920s. The Provident Co-operative Society in Annan was formed in 1872, and by 1956 Annan Co-op had 3,251 members. The Annan Co-op closed in May 2000. In 2003 this building, at the corner of Greencroft Wynd, is being modified to accommodate a new police station.

HIDDLESTON, SADDLERS

Their business was situated at 84 High Street. John Kerr had a similar saddlers shop at 41 High Street which was still in business until about 1976 when the Police Station was built on the site. Miss Kerr hand-sewed saddles and harnesses and other leather goods. The Kerr business had a similar window display to that in the photograph. The small model horses showing their products were of great interest to children.

EDGAR, CLOGGERS

Edgar the Cloggers was established in 1898 at 14 Church Street. Up until the 1950s clogs were the preferred footwear on farms and at Cochran's engineering works. The wearer had warm dry feet and had few foot problems. Repairs consisted of cackering, nailing on replacement iron *cackers* (strips of iron). Annan's two clog businesses, Edgars and Richardsons, didn't need to advertise because the sound of clogs on Annan High Street's whinstone setts woke the town in the early mornings.

ROME'S HIGH-CLASS AERATED WATERS.

20045
48

Speciality :

Rome's Dry Ginger Ale of Unsurpassed Quality.

TRY IT.

Non-Intoxicating Wines. Port, Sherry, Ginger, Raspberry, Blackcurrant, &c., &c. Finest in the Trade,

All Goods are manufactured from the Finest and Purest Materials obtainable. ——

Works: **Solway St., ANNAN.**

ROME'S AERATED WATER WORKS
Rome's Solway Street advertisement in Watt's 1904 Handy Guide to Annan proclaimed them as manufacturers of *high class aerated waters in bottles and siphons*. The same advertisement promoted *Rome's bath for dipping sheep* at the same address. A local death attributed to *suicide* was reported in 1878; the man had drunk sheep fly oil!

CO-OP BAKERY

Jim Chalmers and another baker at the Co-op Bakery, Annan in 1928. At that time Annan had four other bake houses. Later the Co-op built a modern bakery in Moat Road on the site now occupied by Lady Well House.

SCAIFE'S GARAGE

Shown here in the late 1930s, Scaife's Garage was located on the High Street where Farm Foods is now situated. An earlier building, the Globe, was a posting inn. Later the hall on the site was a popular venue for socials and whist drives. Scaife's garage forecourt had electric petrol pumps; Dykes' Garage adjacent to the war memorial retained their hand pumps until about 1960.

CENTRAL HOTEL
The photograph was taken at the entrance to the Central Hotel in about 1905/6. The owners of the splendid 1905 30 HP Rolls Royce are believed to be members of the Rothschild banking family who were frequent visitors to Annan during the fishing season. In its hey-day the boot boy from the Central met every train at Annan Station. The Government took control of all licensed premises in 1916 to control the consumption of alcohol during the construction and operation of the Gretna Munitions factory. The Central Hotel was one of the many Annan hotels and inns which came under Carlisle and Gretna State Management Control. Built in 1897, the hotel was returned to private ownership in 1971 when the scheme was denationalised.

SHEEP SALES
Thomson Roddick & Laurie's Sheep Sales in the Butts Street Mart in 1976. The mart closed in 1997 and the site is now occupied by the Safeway supermarket. The first Annan mart was established by James McLean in 1872 in Port Street, where he also built the Albert Hall. Later in 1873 Kirkpatrick's Mart opened in Murray Street. In 1876 the Murray Street Mart was the venue for a travelling circus.

COLTART'S, CHEMISTS

Tom Coltart (left) in the interior of his chemist's shop on the High Street in 1927. Chemists supplied a wide range of *cures*, but these were mostly ineffective until streptomycin and other antibiotics were introduced in the 1940s. Blockbuster Video now occupies part of the site.

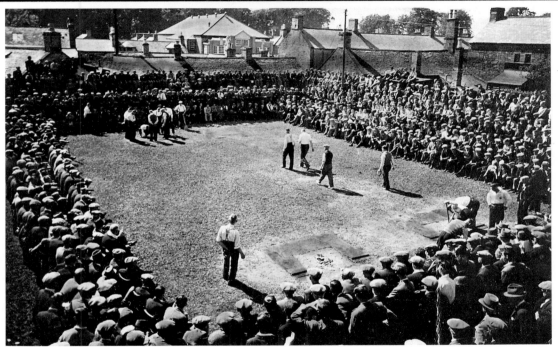

GRACIE'S BANKING

Gracie's Banking was built as a temporary entertainment venue in 1916 by Carlisle and Gretna State Management. It comprised a beer hall with billiards, a restaurant, a cinema, bowling and putting greens and a quoiting pitch. During the 1914-1918 War the State Control rules included *No treating*, which meant you could only buy drink for yourself. On 22 June, 1957 4000 people attended the international Quoiting Match between Scotland and Wales, held at the pitch at Gracie's Banking. Quoiting was a very popular sport, with pitches at Kelhead, Powfoot, Brydekirk and many other villages. William Bone was a prominent member of the Annan Quoiting Club, and later with his wife Doris served Annan Athletic Football Club for more than 45 years.

ELEPHANTS
Elephants in the River Annan around 1900, probably from a circus that partnered Biddall's Show. The North Burn enters the river at this point. This stream, which was an open sewer for many years, was bridged at the bottom of Battery Street in about 1878. It was later contained in a culvert. In times of heavy rain the stream flooded Lady Street (Ladies Well) and part of Butts Street.

BIDDALL FAMILY

The Biddall family were originally travelling showmen who toured fairgrounds. They were famous for *Biddall's Ghost*, which was an illusion using reflections from large glass sheets. They gave lantern slide shows, and in 1898 began showing moving pictures using the newly invented bioscope; this was operated by an electric generator powered by a steam traction engine. The Victor Biddall branch of the family settled in Annan where they operated the *Kinema* at Gracie's Banking from about 1918 until the early 1970s.

BIDDALL'S CLOWNS
Biddall's clowns and an advertisement for their show. This and the two preceding photographs are taken from glass lantern slides which were recovered by chance during house renovations in Annan.

PIGEON RACING

Jim Irving and Eric Johnstone were members of Annan Pigeon Club. In 1959 their bird won the major race which started at Rennes in France. Pigeon racing became popular in the 1900s and Annan & District Homing Club was founded in 1912. Today Annan has about 30 pigeon lofts and many of the racing stock are bred from the very successful strain developed by Johnny Kirkpatrick in the 1940s.

ANNAN AND DISTRICT ATHLETIC CLUB

The Club was formed in 1977, when the above photograph was taken. This group of young runners were being trained by Len Prater, Eddie Dunbar, Stan Austin and John Stevenson and others. The Club organises the popular annual Annan Road Race and the Cross Country River Race to Brydekirk. These races attract runners from all over the district.

SWIMMING AT THE "BIG CREEK"

Annan sewage works was built in the 1950s and produced a foul smell. Remedial work in the 1970s did not remove the odour. During further modifications in 1982 a pipe discharging foul water was let into the *Big Creek*. Up until that time swimming in the Solway at Annan Merse was very popular. This group are enjoying the *Big Creek* at high tide in 1981. Since then few people have used this stretch of shore.

RIDING OF THE MARCHES
The Band and the Fishermen on parade at the Riding of Marches in the early 1900s. Plans are being made to restore the Fishermen's Banner, now in Annan Museum. In 1896 the fishing fleet numbered in excess of 90 boats; by 1956 there were only about fourteen boats. At the present time only one or two boats operate from Annan.

DANCE BAND
During the period following the end of the First World War up to the 1960s, weekly dances were held in many town and village halls. This group in 1969 was one of the many local bands, featuring John Bell drums, Jim Grant trumpet, John Campbell double bass, Russell Bain saxophone and Jack Weild piano.

BLUE ACES
The Blue Aces was one of the larger local dance bands playing in the Victoria Hall Annan in the 1950s. *Back row* John Campbell, Logan McCall, unknown from Dumfries, Jack Weild. *Front row* Bob Robson, Jim Grant, Alan Irving, Irving Caldwell, Dave Garroway.

RIDING OF THE MARCHES

British Nuclear Fuels Chapelcross float in the 1962 Annan Riding of the Marches with Brenda Hunter, a male slave, Margaret Lupton, Dorothea Murphy, Jack Collett, Elma Anderson and Sheila McCrae. The Riding of the Marches is an ancient celebration which is held each year during the first week in July. The Cornet and his Lass with a following of about one hundred horse riders check the 14 miles of the Burgh's boundaries. Then a procession is held. In the evening massed pipe bands and the Annan Silver Band give a spectacular finale on the High Street.

DUMFRIESSHIRE RIFLE VOLUNTEERS

The first local militia was formed in 1669, when Annan was required to provide four men. In 1797 the Dumfriesshire Militia was formed to counter the threat of invasion by the French, but were disbanded in 1816 after the battle of Waterloo. The Dumfriesshire Rifle Volunteers were their direct descendants, created in 1860 when Napoleon III was seeking to succeed where the first of that name had failed. Some volunteers saw service in the Boer War, and in 1908 the Rifle Volunteers across Britain became the nucleus of the Territorial Army. The two men in the photograph, presumed to be from Annan, are wearing the Elcho grey uniforms and shakos of the Royal Dumfriesshire Volunteers. The shakos are decorated with a scarlet band and a ball tuft. The shako badge has a crown set on a bugle. Their beards are in the fashion of Abraham Lincoln, President of the USA from 1861 to 1865. This 1860s photograph was taken by Irving and Co., photographic artists, Poplar Place, Annan, and is the only known photograph of this uniform.

ANNAN HILL ROMAN CAMP

The 1.37 hectare Roman temporary camp on Annan Hill was first identified from the air in 1958 by Professor St Joseph. In 1966 Alan Gibbs confirmed its presence by excavation, and in 1985-6 Dr Lawrence Keppie excavated the east gateway and several points on the defensive ditch in advance of housing development. No internal features or dating material were found. The photograph shows archaeologists removing the dark silt filling the ditch.

"AULD ROBIN GRAY"

Auld Robin Gray is the earliest surviving painting by the distinguished artist William Ewart Lockhart RSA RSW. Lockhart was born at Eaglesfield in 1846, and brought up in Bruce Street, Annan by his grandparents John and Janet Lockhart, the models for the two figures on the left of the painting. He excelled at portraiture, landscapes and scenes from Scottish and Spanish history. His huge oil painting of Queen Victoria's Golden Jubilee in Westminster Abbey, commissioned by the Queen, confirmed his reputation as one of the great Scottish artists of the late nineteenth century.

ANNAN ACADEMY CHOIR
This Annan Academy choir took part in the 1947 Dumfries Music Festival.
Back row L to R. Vena Chalmers, June Woodman, Sylvia Boyes, Nellie Sloan, Eileen Bryson, Betty Black, Sheila Calder, Agnes Gibson, Zylpah Woodman, Anne Wightman. *Centre Row L to R*. Jean Noble, Mary Hope, Wilma Irving, Moira Gass, Willie Robertson, Margaret Turnbull, Sarah Halliday, Helen Johnstone, Jean Roger. *Front Row L to R*. Rennie Walker, Nita Haldane, Betty Chalmers, Margaret Irvine, Beth Kirkup, Music Teacher May Telfer, Mary Gunn, Rector William Wallace, Helen Armstrong, Ena Knox, Margaret Martin, Ursula Thomson, David Murdoch.

41

ANNAN ARMY CADETS

The Annan Army Cadet small-bore rifle team who won the large rosebowl team trophy in the Dumfries and Galloway cadet shooting competition in 1945-46. In the same competition Lance Corporal Wellwood Barton achieved the highest individual score and the silver cup is displayed inside the rosebowl. Back row left to right: L/Cpl Billy Gass, L/Cpl Grant Till, Cpl Jim Hannah, L/Cpl Wellwood Barton. Front row left to right: Cpl Dougie Wallace, Sgt Jim Pool, Captain Wellwood Barton, Officer Commanding Annan Company Army Cadet Force, CSM John Wallace, Sgt George Chalmers.

LADS ARMY

Lads Army volunteer Jim Hawkins guarding Galabank Avenue, Annan in 1940. As with the Victorian militia, it was the local volunteers of *Dads Army* during the Second World War who provided an effective deterrent against invasion.

CHURCH STREET, ANNAN.

CUMBERLAND TERRACE

Cumberland Terrace and Church Street in the 1900s. Cumberland Terrace was built in sandstone in 1852 by John Jackson, who also had a brick and drainage tile works at Shawhill. He built his own large house *Solway Bank* with bricks. In 1871 Mrs Paton's girls' school occupied 4 Cumberland Terrace. In 1875 Miss McMaster was also offering a high class education for ladies in Church Place. At about the same time an Infants' Industrial School was operating in nearby Solway Street, while a Ladies' Boarding School in Bank Street was catering for another group.

WHAMMEL BOAT

Although the Solway Viaduct restricted coastal shipping to Port Carlisle. Annan's poke nets were still fished on both the Gowesk (pronounced Gowkie) and Annan sandriggs. The whammel boat beached beside the viaduct in 1930 displays a fine salmon, testimony to the skill of the boat crew of Jack Irving, his sister Jean and brother George from Back of the Hill. The moustached Tom Rule lived at Summergate Cottage, where he had a small market garden and sold honey. The smartly dressed lady on the right is thought to be a holidaymaker.

JOHN BOYD (ENGINEERS) LTD

In 1947 brothers John and Bob Boyd established their engineering works at Hecklegirth on a siding of the railway which had been a link onto the Caledonian Railway. The company, which eventually employed more than 130 people, designed and built materials handling equipment and a range of hydraulic cranes. Their products were internationally famous, and their railway turntable is one of the centrepieces of the National Railway Museum in York. The firm closed in 1985 and the buildings are now used by Kerr Timber Products. The company was progressive and established a pension scheme for their employees. In the photograph John Boyd (left), founder and Manager of John Boyd Engineers (Annan) Ltd, has presented the firm's first retirement pension cheque to James J Carruthers (centre) who retired after 20 years service. Foreman Robert Thomson (right) presents the gift from the staff.

CARLYLE'S PLACE, JOINER'S SHOP
John S Irvine working in 1961 in G and A Black's joiners shop in Carlyle's Place. The business was started in 1908 in Mafeking Place, and in 1968 employed 29 tradesmen. It closed in 1983. Today B and G Windows own the workshops and manufacture a range of windows and doors.